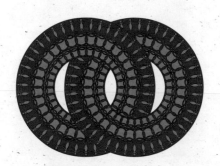

American Rhapsody

American Rhapsody

POEMS

CAROLE STONE

CavanKerry ❖ Press LTD.

CavanKerry Press Ltd.

Fort Lee, New Jersey

www.cavankerrypress.org

Library of Congress Cataloging-in-Publication Data

T/K

Cover photograph by Duquet Design

Cover and interior design by Gregory Smith

First Edition 2012, Printed in the United States of America

CavanKerry Press is proud to publish the works
of established poets of merit and distinction.

CavanKerry Press is grateful for the support it
receives from the New Jersey State Council on the Arts.

Other Books by Carole Stone

Lime and Salt (East Hampton, NY: Carriage House Press, 1997)

Traveling with the Dead (Omaha, NE: Backwaters Press, 2007)

for Harold,
our children,
and our grandchildren

Particularly in America . . . the extraordinary thing is how people . . . fulfill their promises . . . buoyed up by an inevitable destiny.

—F. Scott Fitzgerald

Contents

Contents

American
Rhapsody

I

Invocation/Intoxication

Oak barrels, hops and yeasty brew.
Answer the door for merrymakers
  rushing to get sozzled,
  tasty booze
flowing from kegs, basement jugs.

In bathtubs, in stills—
  poteen, bathtub gin,
  moonshine, apple jack, mountain dew,
  sacramental wine—

  Blue skies, smiling at me

bottles emptied, thrown on garbage heaps from
  nightclubs, saloons and speakeasies
  gin mills, whoopee parlors
new generation of moneymakers roaring
  their Twenties.

It's here at last! Now for a new era of clean thinking and clean living. The Anti-Saloon League wishes every man, woman and child a Happy Dry Year, and a share of the fruits of prosperity which are bound to come with National Prohibition.

On our side of the Hudson
  across from the big-time
racketeers, past the Hoovervilles
beneath the Pulaski Skyway,

on bays and inlets of the New Jersey shore
    the Prohibition high-seas operation
transported cases
of Haig & Haig, Piper Heidsieck, Booth's Gin
from England, France, Scotland
to St. Etienne, Canada and on

    Nothing but blue skies do I see

to just beyond
the twelve-mile limit off Sandy Hook,
the New Jersey Rum Runway,
where men transferred
them from fast skiffs to a fleet
of World War I Mack Bulldog trucks.

The chief business of the American people is business.

Invocation brewing
in my intoxicated imagination,
    the cocktail and I are born!

Father's Voice

How dry I am, how dry I am.
Nobody knows how dry I am.

—Fred Hall

Was your voice rough as scrap metal?
    Did you say "ain't" and "youse"?
A man who only finished fourth grade,

whose mother couldn't read or write,
        did you hire a tutor to help you speak
like the crème de la crème?

To be invited to penthouse parties,
    mingle with high society.
When you came home at dawn,

drunk, did you sing as you slid
    into bed beside mother?
With slurred speech, say the names

of showgirls you slept with?
        Tootsie, Cheri, Bubbles.
Did the mayor you put into office,

who let police sirens scream,
   escorting trucks to warehouses,
Scotch stashed, praise your setting up

soup kitchens, sometimes filling bowls
   yourself, chatting with the hungry
who voted for the politicians

you bribed? Years later they remembered
   that, unlike skinflint Hoover,
you offered a meal.

In Time to Miss America's Long Hangover

Had a little drink about an hour ago.

—James Campbell and Reginald Connelly

Show me the way to go home.
>In apartment basements, town houses,
>>lofts' back rooms, dance studios,

speakeasies hidden away
>in offices, cellar dives, construction
>>sites, even across

from the police station, even right under
>the cops' noses, everyone drank.
>>The setup: a bucket

of ice, glasses, soda water. Order:
>ginger ale, bootleg liquor
>>brought out later, under

a white cloth dinner napkin, alcohol added
>in the kitchen bar.
>>But life began, in America,

the Beautiful, lapping up booze
    after dark, the let's
        live-it-up, out-of-control.

The mirrors covered,
    women howling,
        my father's body beneath a sheet,

the party's over when you least
    expect it.
        I'm tired and I want to go to bed.

IV

The Stranger in the Photo of My Parents

You look happy; your glass is full.
Why are you there, between my parents
in Sloppy Joe's Bar in Habana, in 1935?
My father's associate?

Partner in rum-running?
An IRS man, tracking cash
that went to Batista? A member of a rival clan,
making sure you got your cut?

Just a salesman on vacation
at Cuba's Varadero Beach?
I snipped you out of my copy.
I don't know your name.

Your secrets are buried
in Habana in a bar.
In Cuba, *mi amor.*

V

Running Boards

Take me riding in your car, car.

—Woody Guthrie

Who remembers running boards when a man
      could stand, one foot perched,
      peer down
the blouse of his neighbor's wife,

her hand touching his naked arm.
    Or the way girls sat on the running boards,
    trading secrets until,
leaving for work, he shooed them off to school?

Tiptoe, a girl stepped
    on the running board of her father's Packard,
    turned her cheek for a kiss.
"I'll be back soon," he called, driving off.

I'll take you riding in my car.
    In late afternoon she paced the front stoop.
    Miles away, the windshield splintered,
the radio stopped like his heart.

VI

By the Light of the Silvery Moon

The Chickering piano, the best
that rum-running money could buy.
Carved legs, hand-painted roses
on a yellow background, half-covered

by a flowered fringed shawl,
my father bought so my mother could pass
the evenings alone. War over,
stock market up, in a speakeasy

high rollers hoisted glasses
of single malt, $10.00 a shot,
a month's rent.
Making whoopee!

Piano that holds the photograph
of my parents, sitting close,
that no one plays
that I sat beneath,

I want to spoon,
learning to tie my shoelaces,
listening to the grownups
who never spoke my father's name.

VII
Racketeer Wife

Yes, we have no bananas. We have no bananas today.

—Frank Silver and Irving Cohn

"This is your mother
on the front stoop of 9 Keer.
We had to make her bundle up
in the raccoon coat
and pull the cloche
over her ears. I wrapped
the afghan around her legs.

We told her not to marry him,
but she wouldn't listen,
mad for him. She had everything,
a cook, nanny for you kids, chauffeur,
three cars, a mink, trips to London, Paris.

What good was it, living with a man
with no morals who beat up
his own brother-in-law?

After your father died, your mother
let herself get run down.
We had to fatten her up
with bananas, eggnogs, creamed soups.

We didn't think she'd grieve like that.
She had to wait for him, all hours.
While he could do anything he wanted to.
At the end she was afraid of him.

Maybe that's why she went out
in that terrible rainstorm.
She wasn't thinking straight,
a widow with two kids.
Just a couple of days
and her temperature reached 105.

You look just like her. Thin.
And with those high cheekbones
we all envied."

VIII

Incantation

Little white flowers will never awaken you.

—Resso Seress

Sometimes I feel I could speak
a lost language, the way as a girl

in department stores I would trail
two chatting women through lingerie,

eavesdropping on their Hungarian,
as if, those sounds,

dimly remembered, like an incantation,
would make my mother appear.

And sometimes syllables bubble
from my weeping mouth like water,

making first helpless utterances
that call forth a mother's love.

IX

My Father's Chauffeur

We'll soon be free when the Lord will call us home.

—African-American spiritual

You're my best gal, James Wilson crooned,
telling me how hunger followed him
from Georgia, how he would climb
on the bronze lap of Abraham Lincoln
at the Newark courthouse, where my father found him
polishing lawyers' shoes, and James whispered
in the Great Emancipator's ear, *Set me free.*

He waited in the cold at 3 a.m.
wiping down the white Caddy while my father drank
with women in blue fox fur.
I wanted to go along the April they drove
all the way to Montreal,
my father's money belt fat with bills
for buying whiskey. Sundays,

James took me joyriding round and round
the park's marble-hard lake. We would stop
and feed white bread to the mallards,
then warm ourselves inside the boathouse.

Once he let me sit up front doing 70 miles
over the Pulaski Skyway past squatters' shacks,
the stink of Secaucus in the sky,
the radio mumbling. In the dark
of the back seat, my father's Corona glowed.

James and Mr. Harry

O, what mourning. . . .

—old plantation hymn

Almost eight years old, but James still called me
his *best gal* when he stopped by,
hugging me and letting me sit on his lap.
Your auntie's just plain mean,
he whispered, as she gave him dirty looks.
Maybe she doesn't know any better.
But that's a poor excuse.

James told me stories
about when he was my father's chauffeur,
like being in Newark
the day Dutch Schultz got shot at the Palace Bar.
He said there were cops everywhere,
asking questions, but he told them
he didn't see a thing.

That was the same year he drove my father
to the cemetery. *This time, Mr. Harry*—
that's what he called him—
was the one in the box
and to this day I can't figure out
why you and your brother were kept at home,
he said, his voice getting low,
his arms holding me tighter.

17

It wasn't like the funeral I know,
no singing or stomping,
only weeping and wailing.
No holding your mother's hand.
I thought she was going to throw herself
into his grave.

Marathon Dancing

Ladies and gentlemen, how long can they last?

—master of ceremonies

We sleep on each others' shoulders.
Feet and legs swollen,
shoes worn, we rest until
the whistle starts, marathon not over

yet. For 25 cents they watch
and we have our chance
to win hundreds of dollars.
To keep up the dance,

we shuffle, knit or I sometimes
write letters on a folding desk
around my neck. As long as
my feet don't rest

but move up and down.
We gather nickels and dimes
from the hardwood floor, silver showers
that won't make the time

go any faster. I can't slap my partner awake.
What money we'd make
if we'd waltz or foxtrot! What it takes
to still hunger's ache.

XII

Le Jazz Hot

—for Josephine Baker

In *Revue Nègre,*
face painted, banana skirt
circling her swinging hips,
behind jiggling on cue.

On screen, bare breasts
covered with coral necklaces,
feathered hair, a bright parrot,
swinging on a vine.

In cafés, eyes rolling,
flashing teeth, mock smile,
dancing to *le jazz hot*
with white men.

Far from rioters
who lynched, stoned,
scorched East St. Louis,
sky black with ash,

where she hid in a basement.
Scared girl.
Mad to be herself.
One who got away.

XIII

Rhapsody in Blue

Gershwin bends over the Steinway,
huge orchestra behind him. Ira, backstage,
hums along, unaware of the tumor
squeezing his brother's brain.

He's got the blues, them there blues,
he thinks when George misses notes,
bowing too low until the clapping dies.
Afterwards, brownstone parties

where he pounds the piano keys until dawn.
'S wonderful. It's awfully nice. It's Paradise.
How crazy, how sad
Gershwin should die at thirty-nine.

At ten, swaying
to Paul Whiteman's orchestra
on the tinny Victrola my parents left me,
rhapsody and mourning mix.

Let's call the whole thing off.

XIV
Bundled Hundreds

America the golden! With trick and money damned,
we love thee bitter land.

—William Carlos Williams

If my father hadn't died so soon
after Repeal, would he have, like his partners,
put his money into auto dealerships,

cigarette vending machines, trucking companies?
Moved from Newark to South Orange where
I'd have become a spoiled American princess?

Doc Stacher opened casinos in Habana
and in Las Vegas when it was desert,
each turn of the roulette wheel making him richer.

In England, Joe Reinfeld
became Sir Joseph Renfield,
a Seagram's magnate.

During the Kefauver Hearings, Longie Zwillman
hanged himself. Did the Mob order his death?
Were they afraid he'd talk? A senator asked,

Costello is a big racketeer, isn't he? Longie testified:
If I got to believe what they say about him, then people
will believe what they say about me, so I am not believing it.

22

Would my father have taken the Fifth?
I grew up on bundled hundreds
that the IRS never found.

XV
Great Riches Shall Be Yours

Ernesto is learning
that in America
you have to keep inventing yourself.

> *Immigrant laborers in Palisades Park, New Jersey, say*
> *two days of work at $90/day is a good week.*

One day you're laying sheet rubber
on a leaky flat roof, the next
you are hiring
your undocumented Cuenca cousins.

Rags-to-riches.
American story
we love to believe in.

Like the CEO in pin stripes and tie
who raised his right hand and swore
he didn't know that his financial officer
padded profits, concealed debts,
even after his accountant testified,

> *Under certain business exigencies*
> *I have known Mr. Lay not to tell the truth.*

And my father who, during Prohibition,
paid off motorcycle police
to lead Mack trucks down Broad Street
past Newark's City Hall,
his whiskey in cardboard cartons labeled:
MARMALADE.

Whose riches I fantasize
sit in a numbered Swiss bank account,
in trust for me.

XVI
Choice

Tonight on Lincoln Road, all Miami out,
couples strolling arm in arm, a waiter mambos
to my table, singing, *Mi querida*.

I think of you, Maria, back in New Jersey,
black hair rolled back into a bun,
sipping Cuban coffee, then teetering into the crowd

in your open platforms, polka-dot dress,
your body glistening with its woman's sex,
the way it does when you come late to my class.

Once more I am high on your street-smart poems,
dizzy from your gothic fonts, lost
in your random punctuation. "Call her *abuela*

in your poem," I urge. "Never lose your Spanish."
"So hard to choose the right word," you say.
I recall my own grandmother, who wanted me.

"I would never let her bring you up,
ignorant greenhorn," my aunt said,
"can't read or write English."

But she visited every Sunday with dollar bills
and spearmint gum to stuff into my pockets.
"So pretty like your mother was," she told me.

XVII
So I've Been Told

Grandfather Frederick served the Emperor
polishing hussars' boots. So
I've been told. He died in a New Jersey
mental ward, so a cousin thinks.

Grandmother Katya read Ferenc Molnar
in Hungarian from the Carteret library
and died of a tumor in her belly,
so they tell me. In the old country,

they lived in a mud village no one remembers.
But they said the pears were sweeter than here,
so juicy the Emperor rode out
on his white horse to pick them.

And I have her look, everyone tells me.
One pear of ancestral certainty.

XVIII
Weequahic Park

Named by the hunters and gatherers
    who first fished here,
vanishing without mourning rites,

where my father dressed like a gentleman
    in a plaid cap and knickers,
silver flask in his pocket,

played eighteen holes on Essex County's
    public course when the WASP-only
country clubs wouldn't let him join

and Jamaicans, homesick for island green,
    now bat cricket balls. Park Olmsted designed.
I could lie in its mossy green, run around

the giant lake, its waters sometimes turbulent,
    ice-skate when the lake froze,
buy hot chocolate in the boathouse café.

In the spring I could cast for small carp,
    chase butterflies and spot my first naked man,
lolling in the sun back when hoboes tramped

the railroad tracks to the next camp for work
    or a handout. Where I found
my parents' initials, *H + M,* in a heart

carved on a tree next to EDUARDO Y ISABEL.
     Weequahic Park, whose pines still stand,
age rings hidden in their trunks.

XVIX
Holland Tunnel

What was the land like when the Hudson
kept New York and New Jersey separated
                and the Leni Lenape lived in open air?

Before the Dutch sailed looking for trade,
the Hudson River ferry came,
                and Clifford Holland built the tubes

that, even with their ventilation design, suffocated.
What was the shoreline like
                before its inlets were filled

and Turtle Bay was real? On the gridlocked drive,
exhaust fumes choke. I imagine a forest
                where, on moonlit nights,

a medicine man calls and we leap and dance—
our dead down from their trees—
                by blazing fires, warm and loved.

At the Canal Street exit, the tunnel's dirty tiles
shine in sunlight, and for a moment,
                sorrow disappears.

Harding Terrace

Not nostrums but normalcy.

—Warren G. Harding

No one remembers that the street
I lived on as a child was named
for that country boy, Warren G. Harding
from Blooming Grove, Ohio,
twenty-fourth President of the United
States.

He of the Teapot Dome scandal,
the poker games in back rooms,
stale cigar smoke lingering,
the little house on G Street
where he kept his mistress. He who,

in the special President's dining car,
toasted his cronies with Rhenish wine
in a crystal goblet, eating king crabs
in butter (tainted, it was rumored)
on gold-rimmed china, then,

as the train pulled into San Francisco,
the tip of a last cigar
glowing, lay down
in shame, forever.

 XXI
Home Coming

He used to be a big shot.

—*The Roaring Twenties*, 1930 movie

My father is
a roller coaster, a grey fedora,
cut-glass decanters with silver tags

engraved: *Scotch Gin Rye.*
He missed the 1939 World's Fair,
the War, DiMaggio's fifty-six-game

hitting streak. Free love, the McCarthy Hearings.
His obituary isn't in the archives
of the *Newark Evening News.*

Google can't recover him.
Threads woven into a funeral shroud,
unraveled nightly, that Penelope began again,

waiting for Odysseus. Albeit twenty years late,
he showed up. Only his dog
knew who he was.

XXII

On This Date

In today's *Star Ledger* under On This Date,
Newark's gangsters break up a Bund rally
in Irvington, bloodying the faces of men

who sing *Deutschland über alles*
and stretch their hands high
to shouts of *Sieg Heil!* I see my father
leading the charge.

     Hooray for the good ole USA,
     for the true blue
     Jersey coppers, bribed to stay away,
     while in a land of milk and honey,

     my father uses his fists against evil,
     making this *(Write it!)*
     racketeer's daughter proud.

XXIII
Here's Looking at You

Rob Roys, Bacardis, Gimlets, Sour Rye.
Down the hatch, revelers shout, raising their drinks
along with you, Father, to whom I never said goodbye.

Customers give the password through a door slot, *Joe sent me by*,
and after a couple of rounds of liquor, they're *in the pink*.
Rob Roys, Bacardis, Gimlets, Sour Rye.

To a long life and a merry one or *Here's mud in your eye*!
America's dark heart parties as rich and poor think
along with you, Father, to whom I never said goodbye,

the good times will never end. No one told me why
you left or where you went. Your ice-cubed glass clinks.
Rob Roys, Bacardis, Gimlets, Sour Rye.

For in this scenario you will never die,
still at the bar flirting with peroxide wives in minks.
I leave you in limbo, Father, to whom I never said goodbye,

dapper in solid cream pants and regimental tie.
Here's looking at you, a man forever linked
with Rob Roys, Bacardis, Gimlets, Sour Rye.
Father, goodbye.

XXIV
Instead of Father, I Have Uncles

My uncle, Mother's brother,
beheads chickens. Their blood
spouting, he digs into the cavity
for the tiny yellow unborn eggs.
He calls his geese
my little ones, pushing bread crusts
down their throats.

The half-uncle, born to Grandmother late,
a grown man who reads comics,
whom the neighborhood kids named *Four Eyes,*
pulls the wings off insects; I hide
when he rings the doorbell, afraid
of his crossed eyes, his kiss,
how he presses his tongue against mine.

Sundays at the China Clipper,
my 300-pound guardian uncle
cracks a lobster claw. When
he puts his arm around me,
his fat fingers pressing my shoulder,
I feel his chest heat, the loose flesh
beneath his armpits, the heavy grip
I can't break.

XXV

Periwinkles

Heaped in pails, the periwinkles
a schoolgirl hawks above this Irish strand
have the briny smell of the seaside town
where I made up a mother

who told me a bedtime story
before she drifted off to a party
with my tuxedoed father. They left me
their trunk stuffed with secrets,

peeling stickers: Hotel Connaught, the Shelborne.
How easily Jameson whiskey must have gone down
his throat while she took tea;
later, were there Galway Bay oysters

on toast points in hotel dining rooms
under giant chandeliers?
Did Mother glitter, ballroom dancing?
Did Father chalk a billiard stick?

"Push this pin in," the girl says,
"and then, ever so carefully, pull a winkle out."
Wet with the sea.

XXVI
Boardwalk

We envy those who loved their childhood
since we didn't love ours,
except for the rind of boardwalk

with its custard stands and penny arcades
where we paced behind strolling uncles
who replayed pinochle hands while aunts argued

whether cherrystones or littlenecks
were sweeter for chowder. After nor'easters
stripped the beach we hunted

for nickels and dimes,
the ocean foam like milkshake
bubbles we made with straws. Boys snapped

beach towels at us, girls nicknamed
Honey and Cookie. Our brothers
covered us up to our necks

in sand that stuck
to our hair, our eyes,
the waves lapping at our buried feet.

We envy those
who never had to dig themselves out
so they could run away.

XXVII
Assaults

Szymborska has won the Nobel.
At outdoor cafes in Krakow,
the young Szymborska wrote on menus
with a fountain pen. Maybe she wore a beret,
let her hair fall in a mane. Cavalry officers
cantering by sighed when they saw her.

Summers we rented in Asbury Park,
three families in one house, and me, the orphan,
stuck with them. In the bungalow in back
for the low-life in-laws, during the all-night-fight,
Bessie of the three chins threw a frying pan
at her husband Benny, the plumber.
The police came; what greater disgrace?

So I let Szymborska, forever young like my mother,
stroll the Baltic seaside, the smell
of roasting chestnuts mingling with the sea air,
when Gdansk was Danzig.

XXVIII
Gates

On wide porches above the boardwalk,
    Christian women with blue-rinsed hair
    rock in hotels' wicker chairs.
On our way to
    cotton candy, pinball machines, ski-ball,
    we hurry past before the town gates
    slam shut like orphanage doors.
We can see
    the Ferris wheel and funhouse lights
    shining from the next beach town
    like new planets.
At the cobwebbed miniature Bethlehem,
    open all year, the carved virgin's wooden face
        stares at us, her peeled painted arms
        clasping her baby.
From a white steeple church,
    chords of "Jesus Loves You"
    speed toward us, children of a hard God
    who sends plagues.

XXIX
Goodbye, Kate Smith

Our parents left the dishes in soapy water
to listen to your voice boom *God Bless America*

over airwaves into our Magnavox.
Goodbye to our dream of one people

from the mountains to the prairies to the oceans
we believed in while all the world warred.

Gone, too, the cherry bottled soda
and July suppers at the Jersey shore,

kids at one table, trading *Wonder Woman*
for *Captain Marvel* while grownups at another

dissolved in clouds of Lucky Strike.
The opal moon still shines on the boardwalk,

rotting now, on the shuttered funhouse,
on the ocean white with foam.

Mystery Heroines

I'd have a badge.
My code name would be "Blondie"
and I'd act like a moll.
I'd go undercover to get to the Mob,
find the killers, testify at their trials,
risk being buried
with garbage in the Meadowlands.

But wait!
Would I be turning in my father?
I'm no fink!

I'd wear a blue cloak,
resuscitate patients on the late shift
when no doctor was around,
take a mercy flight,
get the antidote to the dying wife,
her husband pacing as the plane
is almost torn apart in cloudy turbulence.

In the real-life scenario,
it's my mother who's sick
and there is no antidote,
penicillin not yet discovered.

Hurrah for America's heroines!
For Sue Barton, for Nancy Drew!
Hurrah for me!
Our whole bright lives ahead.

XXXI
There Ain't No Santy Claus

A bulky Brinks armored car
speeds past other cars on the road.
        Does it hold cash?
I remember those thirties movies with masked

stick-up men who hijacked Brinks,
        carrying off hundreds of thousands.
The rat-a-tat-tat of Tommy guns
filled the theatre as we cheered,

moved by their daring,
licorice blackening our teeth.
        O for the chase,
the sirens, the narrow escape.

In the fadeout scene, under the high-vaulted ceilings,
a grey-faced husband signed a contract
        in a bank hushed as a church
that put his family forever in search

of a way to pay back debt. Now Brinks veers
onto the crowded Parkway as, once more,
        banks and corporations broke,
we curse that old god Mammon, for in a stroke,

we can't pay what we owe,
make a gangster a hero.

XXXII
Don't Touch That Dial!

Who has figured out why Joe Penner,
radio star no one knows now,
made us laugh, asking a million times,
Wanna' buy a duck?

But like all the figures
we worshipped, he didn't really help.
Hollow, they couldn't save the world:
Buck Rogers whom we wanted to follow
into space, the Lone Ranger, masked man,

fighting injustice in the Old West,
Hi-yo, Silver,
the Green Hornet who went after criminals
G-men couldn't find. Because the dial
we touched, warm from the radio tubes,

couldn't stop evil
from lurking in the hearts of men.
The Shadow taught us this.
And we can't pretend.

XXXIII

Bergen Street

This land is your land.

—Woody Guthrie

"Bergen Street babe," we called Aunt Sylvia
(not really our aunt) with her peroxide hair, chain smoking,
red lipstick that stained her coffee cups, shoulder pads.
Saturdays when she showed up for the all-day Mah-Jongg game,
and chucked us under the chin rasping, "Sweetheart," we ducked.
When she imitated Mrs. Roosevelt's high squeaky voice,
snapped open her snake-skin bag,

we knew
        we'd wear peasant skirts,
        turn vegetarian,
        already becoming women
        who, at Pete Seeger concerts, would sing ourselves hoarse
        to save the Lordly Hudson

                    This land is my land

while,
far from Bergen Street
in a Miami Beach Old Ladies Home,
she cried out,
"One Bam, two Crack."
White hair thin, lips pale.

            This land was made for you and me.

XXXIV
Beauty Parlor

Yvette's on Grove Street is still here,
chic as a tail-fin car,
with hairdryers and old shampoo sinks
that make your neck feel unscrewed
when you lean back.
> *The water's too hot,*
> *now, too cold.*

Over customers' toweled heads,
the owner's voice declares,
> *Yeah, my lottery ticket was one number off.*
> *A five mil' pot.*
> *Can you believe it?*

TV's always on to *Oprah*
or a Sinatra movie.
> *Frankie could have put his shoes*
> *under my bed anytime.*

As they did when young marrieds,
thin-haired old ladies come,
pushing their walkers with flair.
> *Did you hear Josie Ryan died?*
> *I knew her forty years.*
> *She should have taken Lipitor*
> *like I told her.*

Today a woman is celebrating
her sixtieth wedding anniversary.
Shrouded in back plastic,
she cranks herself up
from the faucet's hot water.
>   *We're going to Tony's Place for dinner.*
>   *Don't want to get too excited.*
>   *Just happy to be alive.*

History

I thought I would never become bourgeois.
Now I watch *Nightly Business Report*
the way some watch *Oprah,*

shift stocks to bonds then back again
in my Deferred Comp Plan,
worrying about the Fed's next move.

My dream of America,
where no one would be poor,
slipping away into history.

XXXVI
Full House

Another inscrutable house.

—Elizabeth Bishop

Friday nights I play poker.
Penny-ante games.
I deal the cards,
hoping for a full house.
With only a pair of tens, I am lost.
Yet a failed hand is hardly trouble.

There is more serious trouble
than failing at poker.
Elizabeth Bishop lost
her parents, her lover Lota's games
and Brazilian house.
Too many bad cards.

But this isn't just about cards.
As a girl I, too, found trouble.
To escape from my aunt and uncle's house,
I danced naked, an under-the-boardwalk game,
my eleven-year-old version of strip poker,
trying to forget what I had lost.

It's a childhood of being lost
after the king and queen become lifeless cards,
like the small girl in *Forbidden Games,*
parents killed by a German plane. Such trouble
is godless poker.
Now the girl lived in a stranger's house,

the way I grew up in someone else's house.

She secretly buried lost
mice that died. A movie can be like real-life poker.
After first grief you must master the cards.
But that movie is about old trouble,
and I am tired of forbidden games,

would rather play happy games
Who cares if you don't hold a full house?
Is this really trouble?
Though in deal after deal I lost,

there's more to worry about than cards.
So every Friday I leave ruthless life for poker,

no longer lost. If life is like a game
of cards, let the trouble be
Friday-night poker at someone's house.

XXXVII
Cigars

What this country needs is a good five cent cigar.

—Thomas Riley Marshall

My father held a Corona Gigante
casually with three fingers.

My guardian uncle carried a short Churchill
in his mouth, wet, never lit.

Castro waved a Bolivar Fino like a flag,
bragging about power.

I loved to puff a cigarillo in the West Village
like "Vincent" Millay. Inhaling desire.

XXXVIII
FDR

We grew up thinking "Roosevelt"
meant "President." Term after term,
his pince-nez portrait watched over us
from our schoolroom walls. We gathered

by the radio, our hearth, to hear
his silver voice call us "Friends."
In movie houses, we cheered him, believing
he was perfect, standing before Congress,

braced legs hidden, the Commander-in-Chief,
the parent who would keep us safe.
When that train, a god's chariot,
carried him from Warm Springs back

to Washington, the black box wrapped
in the Stars and Stripes, we waited for him
at railway crossings, looking for the father
we believed in, childhood ending.

XXXIX
In Newark

Three young men and a young woman, off to college
in September, gang members force to kneel
    against a wall, holding guns to their heads,

murdered in a school yard. A seven-year-old boy,
driving with his mother.
    shot by men speeding by in a car.

A truant ninth grader giving birth
in a car lot stifles her baby's cry.
    From Frelinghuysen to McCarter Highway,

Clinton Avenue to Lyons, death patrols the streets,
loiters among the jobless in Military Park.
    School kids aren't taught the Presidents,

the ex-mayor is found guilty of stealing.
In the city where George Washington began
    his march to the Delaware,

ache for those I lost
never stilled, I memorized the states
    in alphabetical order, under Lehigh Avenue's

leafy trees played two-hand touch football,
lived in a house no one told me I owned,
    deeded by grandmother with an X.

Where skyways and turnpikes begin
the crossing of America,
        in the Osborne Terrace Library,

Icarus not yet fallen from the sky,
I found my first poets, pastoral all,
        the gift that saved me.

XL

English-American-Duet

i Silly

The uncle who toiled for Esso in smoky Perth Amboy,
its oil refinery tanks lining Route One,
cursed the bosses after too many whiskeys.
"Why do you want to write poetry?" he asked.
"It's silly, words won't change a thing."
Today, at Nenthead, an art exhibit
mourns the used-up veins,
where men once mined for lead.
Alongside a photograph of Northumbrian men
who breathed in fumes, W. H. Auden's lines,
Sickly standing, their eyes like drugged rabbits,
remember the miners of his North England youth.
They had the Pennines for delight,
unlike my uncle, without a crag in sight.

ii Lenny

"They're playing Bernstein's *West Side Story*
today. Terribly glitzy." Overheard chatter
in high-toned Oxford accents, as we queue
at 10 a.m. for Holy Well Concert tickets.
I want to say, "Give him a break,"
as if they had insulted an uncle.
We file in to hard benches,

a white room, plain as a Quaker
meeting house. *Founded in 1643,*
the sign outside reads, America not yet free.
"What will you do for the hols?"
"Bicycle in France." "Lovely."
Tuning up, a cello, a violin. Lenny,
squiggling like a saxophone, pushes himself in.

XLI
The Past

The past swings
a noose from a tree,

you do not let its rope
    tighten,

getting ready for a new fiction
possible at a certain age.

The past wears away
    gradually

until nothing is left
but yourself.

XLII
Rooftop

The mystery of blue
rooftop minarets, the Pacific beyond,
just as I imagined. In the distance,
two palms. Over my head, a flock

of gulls in formation flop
their way north, returning
to their first nesting place. How can I
reach my mother and father?

He's embalmed in whiskey. She's shrouded
in silver. They're not
in the sky, on land
or in the sea.

They row in me, jostling
my son, my daughter, my two granddaughters.
I won't let them
crowd my loves out.

XLIII
Inky Heart

I turn a corner,
see my parents down the
street,
    they who turn up
    everywhere.

I wave to them,
    as long-lost friends.

My lips form their names.
I say them as an invocation—
    Margaret, Harry—

they who live
as language
    in my inky heart.

XLIV
Home: Ceremonies

i

Overnight, forsythia by the roadside,
by the hillside, beneath the underpass.
Bach on the radio. *Nicht! Nicht! Jesu! Jesu!*

rattles rooftops. Betrayal in the Garden.
How quickly the yellow
will vanish, as if it had never come.

ii

Who are we when we speak
the bone, when we dig
in the sky? Who are we

when we bow to nothing,
no, not anyone?
Yet, moon hanging and oh, stars.

iii

What she wants is to wade knee-deep
in tenderness, to swim in that river,
her dearest ones holding her.

She gathers yellow flowers for the ceremony.
Which could be emptiness.
Which could be wholeness.

XLV

Root

There's a hole in my heart,
a place where the dead hide
in their secret clubhouse.

How chatty they are
as they smoke their cigarettes
and pretend to be alive.

I can't touch them or speak
to them, can only hear
their laughter like chimes

and light candles.
They have taken all they thought
and said with them,

leaving me
to search for their chronicles.
Mouths without breath,

they don't care
how I continue
tough as a root.

XLVI
Black Dress

Can I give my black dress to Goodwill?
It's like my dream of the sea.
Can I kiss it goodbye?
I wore it for Uncle Sid's funeral, sitting
among the acquaintances in the back row.

No one said I was the child he helped raise.
He had kidney stones, diabetes, carried a fat belly,
and ate at the kitchen table, white napkin
hugging his throat. His mother and father,
first cousins, married in the old country.

Every day I was grateful I wasn't cursed
with his blood, though he never complained
that he took me in. Once he brought back
saltwater taffy and a giant Mr. Peanut bar
from Atlantic City where he won at blackjack.

I wanted to know what it was like on the Steel Pier
with the ocean lapping beneath it.
My dream was to live near water,
to smell of the sea.

I kept those sweets for months
until they melted like the lozenges
I find weeks later
in the pocket of the dress
I wear to funerals.

XLVII

A Daughter Returns to Her Habana Fantasy

Here I am again, Father, searching
Sloppy Joe's souvenir photo for the man you
were. Cigar between two fingers,
face forever handsome and tan,
the only likeness you left me. Again I wonder,
as you leaned against the bar,

beer bottle half full, one foot on a bar-
stool rung, did you miss me? To search
your dark hair, your flowered tie, is to wonder
if a chorus girl's fishnet legs beckoned you,
kicking across La Tropicana's stage, tan
and taut. Your rum money leaks onto my fingers

that caress the fading photo. Fingers
wanting to be kissed as if I could stand at the bar
smelling your daiquiri breath, touching your tan
face. I want to be embraced, as I search
the humid harbor breezes for you
where rum sailed to the States. Customs bribed not to wonder

what the cargo was. The wondrous
Bacardi marked "cigars" so no one could finger
it to the Coast Guard. I imagine you
with a pin-striped Cuban in his barred
high-ceilinged living room, search-
lights beaming over two men in tandem,

counting bundles of American dollars. His tan-
trum prone wife plays canasta, not yet wondering
when Fidel's guerillas would search
for them, her diamond-ringed fingers
glittering above shiny cards. Barred
windows shattered, what's gone is gone, you,

your cigar smoke, and Batista's, who, like you,
disappeared. Drunk on that city that tantalizes,
its crumbling buildings and tail-finned cars barely
preserved, while Morro Castle, the Spanish wonder,
guards the bay, my fingers
open a rum bottle. Elixir spilled, I search

where the rich search for gated villas in Habana's new wonder-
land. The Nacional's bar reopened, the casino wheel turning
     where you
hit the jackpot, chips gathered up now by tan young fingers.

XLVIII

Edward Hopper:
Outside the Frame

i.

In *The Bootleggers* three men in black
rain slickers power their white skiff

toward a figure standing in front
of a gabled house, almost lost.

They might well be my uncles,
evading the Coast Guard

in quiet Jersey inlets. The one
sketched in on shore,

the sky blank above him,
could be my father,

his whiskey trucks
outside the frame.

ii.

In *Tables for Ladies* a waitress
leans over a row of grapefruit near

a blackboard with specials. The cashier
leans an elbow on the glass

cigar counter. Stiff as mannequins,
a couple stare across their table,

as my parents might have. Maybe
he'll buy a cigar, bite off the end

and then light it, flirt with the cashier,
while she makes change.

iii.

That's the artist's wife by herself again,
wherever her husband set up his easel,

this time seen through a brownstone's window,
wearing a red slip, bare shoulders white

as my mother's were in her peignoir,
waiting up for my father.

Notes

Book epigraph: From F. Scott Fitzgerald, "Majesty," *Saturday Evening Post* (July 1929).

"Invocation/Intoxication": On January 16, 1919, the Eighteenth Amendment of the Constitution of the United States was ratified, stating that in one year it would be prohibited to make, sell, transport, import, or export intoxicating liquors within the United States and its territories. Song lyrics from Irving Berlin, "Blue Skies Smiling at Me," 1927. Lines 16-18, William Anderson, *New York Herald*, January 17, 1920. Line 36 from "Business As the Savior of the Community," *Independent*, April 16,1921.

"Father's Voice": Epigraph from Fred Hall, "How Dry I Am,"1930.

"In Time to Miss America's Hangover": Epigraph and song lyrics adapted from James Campbell and Reginald Connelly, "Show Me the Way to Go Home," 1925.

"Running Boards": Epigraph and song lyrics from Woody Guthrie, "Car Song," 1958.

"By the Light of the Silvery Moon": Title from the song of the same name by Gus Edwards and Edward Madden, 1909.

"Racketeer Wife": Epigraph from Frank Silver and Irving Cohn, "Yes, We Have No Bananas," 1923.

"Incantation": Epigraph translated from Resso Seress, "Szomoru Vassarnap" ("Gloomy Sunday"), 1933, a song that became famous in Hungary after numerous unhappy lovers left suicide notes quoting lines from it.

"My Father's Chauffeur": Epigraph from a spiritual that became famous at the beginning of the Civil War, when South Carolina slaves were jailed for singing words that slave owners believed spoke of freedom and opposition to slavery.

"James and Mr. Harry": Epigraph from William Barton, *Old Plantation Hymns*, 1899.

"Marathon Dancing": Marathon dancing, a 1920s craze, was popular along with other endurance tests such as flagpole sitting. During the Great Depression, when it became a competition for monetary prizes, the dancers were frequently exploited.

"Le Jazz Hot": Stanza 4 refers to the race riots in East St. Louis in 1917, the title to the music performed by black musicians who left America for Paris in the Twenties and Thirties.

"Rhapsody in Blue": Song lyrics from Ira Gershwin and George Gershwin, "'S Wonderful," 1927.

"Bundled Hundreds": Epigraph from William Carlos Williams, *Paterson* (New York: New Directions, 1948), 85. The lines in italics are testimony by Abner "Longie" Zwillman from the *Kefauver Report* (Washington, D.C.: U.S. Government Printing Office, 1951). The men mentioned began as New Jersey rum runners during Prohibition in a group that came to be known as The Syndicate.

"Great Riches Shall Be Yours"; Title from William Carlos Williams, *Paterson* (New York: New Directions, 1948), 66. Lines 4 and 5 from the *Record* [Bergen County, N.J]: August 22, 1994. Lines 19 and 20 are from Mike Muckleroy, Enron trial testimony, May 8, 2006.

"Harding Terrace": Epigraph from Harding's election speech, Boston, May 14, 1920. Teapot Dome was a scandal during his administration. Harding died of an embolism, but it was widely rumored he had been poisoned and had committed suicide.

"On This Date": For the phrase *(Write it!)* I am indebted to Elizabeth Bishop's "One Art."

"Gates": The "gates slam shut" refers to the Methodist Conference Board's 1877 ruling that Ocean Grove's town gates would be closed to cars on Sundays.

"There Ain't No Santy Claus": Title from a line in *Three Godfathers*, a 1936 movie.

"Bergen Street": Epigraph and song lyrics from Woody Guthrie, "This Land Is Your Land," 1940.

"Full House": Epigraph from Elizabeth Bishop, "Sestina," 1965.

"Cigars": The epigraph was a casual comment by Thomas Riley Marshall, vice-president under Woodrow Wilson, made to a clerk during a pause in a senator's 1915 speech.

"English-American-Duet": Line 11, from W. H. Auden, "In the Year of My Youth," 1932, unpublished poem cited in www.MyersNorth.Co.UK. For the phrase "Squiggling like a saxophone" I am indebted to a line in Wallace Stevens's "The High-Toned Old Christian Woman," Harmonium (New York: Vintage Books, 1922), 59.

Acknowledgments

Many thanks to the editors of the following publications in which these poems first appeared:

Chelsea: "Root"
Exit 13: "So I've Been Told"
New Jersey Journal of Poems: "Black Dress"
Poemeleon: "Here's Looking at You"
Southern Poetry Review: "My Father's Chauffeur"
Tiferet: "Home: Ceremonies"
Umbrella: "Edward Hopper: Outside the Frame"

"Running Boards" was published as "Spin" in *Fathers: A Collection of Poems* (New York: St. Martin's Press, 1997). "Weequahic Park" was published in *The Poetry of Place: North Jersey in Poetry* (Paterson, N.J.: Passaic County Community College, Poetry Center, 2008). "Instead of Father, I Have Uncles" was published as "Uncles" in my chapbook *Orphan in the Movie House* (Hartford, Conn.: Andrew Mountain Press, 1997). Several poems, in different versions, appeared in my e-zine chapbook *The Chief Business of Americans* (Chicago: Beard of Bees, 2008).

Thanks to Molly Peacock for her enthusiasm and her insightful suggestions and to Francis Quinn for getting me started and helping me to finish.

CavanKerry's Mission

Through publishing and programming, CavanKerry Press connects communities of writers with communities of readers. We publish poetry that reaches from the page to include the reader, by the finest new and established contemporary writers. Our programming brings our books and our poets to people where they live, cultivating new audiences and nourishing established ones.

Other Books in the Notable Voices Series